Beauty
of
Bath

by
JULIA COOPER

MCMLXXXVI
EUROPEAN LIBRARY - ZALTBOMMEL/NETHERLANDS

Essays reproduced by kind permission of the Bath Evening Chronicle.

LIST OF DRAWINGS BY THE AUTHOR

Sally Lunn's House With Negro Boy, 20

Sarah Siddon's Likeness from Gainsborough Portrait, 25

The Victorian Theatre Royal, 26

Bath Abbey in Churchyard, 32

Royal Crescent with Miniatures after the Rev. and Mrs. George Austen, 41

Sun Temple in Wintry Sydney Gardens, 54

Roman Bath with Diving Stone, 59

Pulteney Bridge in Moonlight Fantasy, 77

Once again Bathonians and visitors will enjoy Julia Cooper's vivid account of the historical buildings and parks in Bath, and share her pleasure discovering the men, women and children who lived with such gifted style in this beautiful city. Try her collection of 60 apple recipes inspired by the apple known as the Beauty of Bath.

GB   ISBN 90 288 3404 4 / CIP

© 1986 European Library - Zaltbommel/Netherlands

No part of this book may be reproduced in any form, by print, photoprint, microfilm or any other means without written permission from the publisher.

Printed and bound by Grafisch Bedrijf De Steigerpoort in Zaltbommel/Netherlands.

CONTENTS

Springtime in Bath	4
The Pump Room	8
I Wonder If The Monk Still Chants	14
The Linley Family	18
The Theatre at Bath	24
Bath Abbey	31
The Guildhall	36
Jane Austen in Bath	39
Assembly Rooms and Yehudi Menuhin	46
3p Shoes Shine in Museum of Costume	50
Winter Wonderland in Sydney Gardens	53
Oratory in the Roman Baths	58
Botanical Gardens	63
Parade Gardens	65
Hunting for Antiques	68
Ghost Hooves Bridge A Chasm of 300 Years	72
Country Stroll in Widcombe	76

SPRINGTIME IN BATH

Citizens blink eyes in bright sunshine and see Bath anew after months of hurrying from one heated building to another. In the squares blossom appears on the trees.

Romantics in springtime see Bath Spa as a city of enchantment, veiled in morning mist, encircled by green hills. After breakfast this light vapour drifts away to reveal streets and crescents of town houses mellow in sunshine. Golden weather vanes on the tower of Bath Abbey gleam as they gently indicate a south-westerly breeze. No wonder a fruit grower in the last century named her new variety of sweet apple the Beauty of Bath.

Bath is one of four places in the world to have a hot mineral spring rising from thousands of feet below the surface. Its soporific warmth fills the air and soothes visitors, when they arrive to escape rigours of their working life. Twice in 2,000 years a highly civilised society has occupied the city.

Romans used the mineral water for Turkish and other types of bathing, so they could relax between fighting. Bath became famous as Aquae Sulis. The Romans' goddess of sewers Venus Cloacina, must have despaired when Saxons invaded the city in 577, and ruined the drainage system, allowing Bath to sink into a smelly, sordid stupor for twelve hundred years! Imagine dead dogs, pigs and people bobbing up and down in the King's Bath. To some citizens the Abbey must have appeared heavenly.

In the 18th century, fashionable Georgians brought another civilised society to Bath, when they realized the hot spring water was medically beneficial. Speculators bought up acres of land in the city, pulled down decaying houses and built elegant estates for visitors to rent.

Bath became a spa resort. Without a town planning committee, Georgian architects, inspired by the classical Palladian style of the Italians, produced brilliant designs for streets, terraces and crescents.

Consequently, gentry were enticed from London for many sparkling seasons, under the watchful eye of Beau Nash.

The title of this book 'Beauty of Bath' is aptly named for not only does it refer to the lovely City of Bath, but to the famous English apple raised by a Victorian grower about 1864. What delight there must have been when the Beauty of Bath apple was awarded a First-Class Certificate by the Royal Horticultural Society in 1887. It remains one of the leading early dessert apples, and is planted in all parts of England.

Since pre-historic times apples have been eaten and the crab varieties are the source of many important cider apples. In Somerset, ancient customs like 'Wassailing' the trees on Twelfth Night are still practised, and associated with cider making.

Dessert and culinary apples were undoubtedly planted by the Romans during their colonisation in Britain, one variety being the Continental Pomme D'Api.

In Bath and the surrounding countryside for many years orchards in blossom have been a sight to behold in spring, later the trees laden with golden and crimson fruit at harvest time.

For your culinary delight I hope you will enjoy this collection of apple recipes.

*

SPICY APPLE DAPPY (Somerset's version perhaps of the Pomme D'Api)

Plenty for 6 people.

Ingredients: 8 oz self-raising flour; 1 teaspoon baking powder; pinch of salt; 2 oz butter; ¼ pt. milk; 1 lb cooking apples; 1 tablespoon demerara sugar; ½ level teaspoon cinnamon, nutmeg, ground cloves or mixed spice.

Syrup: Juice of one lemon; 1 tablespoon golden syrup; ½ oz butter; 4 oz sugar, 7 fluid oz water.

Method: Make syrup first. Peel a fine strip of lemon rind and squeeze lemon. Put rind, juice and all other ingredients in a pan and stir over a gentle heat until sugar is dissolved. Remove from heat and leave in the pan until needed.

Sift flour, baking powder and salt into a bowl. Rub in butter and then mix to a dough with milk. Roll out on a floured board to a rectangle about 8" x 5" and ¼" thick. Peel, core and finely slice apples, and spread on pastry. Mix sugar and spice together and sprinkle over apple. Roll up pastry and apple like Swiss roll. Then cut into slices about 1" thick. Grease an ovenproof dish and lay slices on it. Remove lemon rind from syrup and pour over the apple slices. Bake in a moderately hot oven for about 30 minutes. Gas 6, 375°F.

Serve with cream.

CRAB APPLE AND ROWAN JELLY

Soak the rowan berries in hot water for a day before you begin. Then add a third of their weight in chopped crab apples. Simmer fruit with ½ pint of water to every lb of fruit. Strain for several hours through a scalded jelly bag or strong linen cloth. Do not squeeze the bag or the resulting jelly will be cloudy. Measure the juice back into a saucepan. To every pint add a little lemon and 1 lb of sugar. Stir over low heat to dissolve the sugar, then bring up to a brisk boil. Boil steadily for a set, about 10-15 minutes. When ready draw off the heat and skim thoroughly for a clear sparkling preserve. Pour into clean, warm jars. Cover and seal while hot. Label when cold. This astringent jelly is good with meat.

APPLE FLORENTINE (Florentine is the old word for pie; once called Flory Pie)

Ingredients: Tart eating apples; brown sugar; sultanas; butter for frying; cinnamon; cloves; cider; 1 cup of sugar; packet of frozen puff pastry.
Method: Quarter apples, peel and core. Fry over moderate heat in butter until brown on all sides, and slightly soft. Put into a deep pie dish, scattering brown sugar, sultanas and a little ground cinnamon and cloves between layers. Pack the dish solidly. Pour in a cupful of cider and cover with thinly rolled pastry. Make a hole in the centre to allow steam to escape. Bake in a hot oven for 20 minutes, then turn heat down to 350°F (gas 4) until a skewer pushed through will glide through the apples without resistance — about another 20 minutes.
Dust the crust with icing sugar before serving with cream.

MULLED CIDER (So heartening in wintertime with spices and decorated with fruit)

Serves 10-12.
Ingredients: 2 small eating apples; 6 cloves; generous litre/1 quart still cider; 4 in. stick cinnamon; 2 level teaspoons ground ginger; 2 oz soft brown sugar; ¼ pint water; 1 small orange.
Method: Core apples and break the skin round the centre of each apple with a knife. Stick two cloves in each apple and bake in a moderate oven 350°F (gas 4) for 20 minutes. Meantime

gently heat cider in a saucepan — must not boil. Put remaining 2 cloves, cinnamon broken into 4 pieces, the ginger, sugar and water into a separate saucepan and stir over the heat until sugar has dissolved. Bring to the boil and simmer gently for 5 minutes. Remove from heat. Transfer baked apples to the punch bowl and add the orange cut in slices. Strain the spiced water and then pour in the hot cider. Serve at once.

* * *

To the island valley of Avilion;
Where falls not hail, or rain, or any snow,
Nor ever wind blows loudly, but it lies
Deep meadow'd, happy, fair with orchard lawns
and bowery hollows crown'd with summer sea.
From 'The Passing of Arthur' by Lord Tennyson.

THE PUMP ROOM

Join me now in the Pump Room. Imagine that the early 18th century clock standing at the rear of the room had been built with a concealed tape recorder. Its taped gossip down the years would startle quiet, elderly coffee drinkers here today.
When Thomas Tompion, most famous of all clockmakers, built the long case clock in 1709, society visited the Pump Room to exchange the most scandalous gossip in England!
In 1706, the original Pump Room, completed by Beau Nash, was opened in a blaze of publicity. Society was told of unsurpassed luxury and comforts, including the three and five seater rout benches, we can sit on today. Even the word 'rout' means party of revellers!
Beau Nash wrote: 'In a palatial atmosphere, to the strains of fine music, patrons can enrich their health by drinking glasses of invigorating hot water, always obtainable.'
There was a procession through the city, and a concert in praise of legendary Prince Bladud, who it was believed had discovered the Bath waters with his Keynsham swine.
These Roman Baths were not discovered until 1879. Beau Nash would have been surprised if he had known Romans had built their Baths so near the Pump Room, for he saw only houses, which had their foundations set in the silt that had built up within the Baths themselves.
In 1706 this enterprising Welshman Richard Nash was concerned with his time, not past history. Post boys on horseback rushed news of the Pump Room's opening to London in 22 hours.
Exaggerated accounts of the room with its painted ceiling and minstrel's gallery caused a stir, and Londoners longed to see the city.
At that time amusement differed little from that in vogue under Charles II. Men danced in their thick riding boots, and ladies, including the Duchess of Queensbury, wore aprons.
Beau Nash whipped off the Duchess' apron, politely rebuking her, and he would descend on young men in their boots to en-

quire distainfully: 'Have you not forgotten your horse?'

This amazing Master of Ceremonies forbade men to wear swords in Bath after seeing frequent duels by gamblers in the Pump Room. The losing duelist, having a sword run through his body, caused hysterics among the ladies!

To encourage genteel behaviour, Beau Nash appointed the Pumper, who saw glasses of mineral water were courteously served in the Pump Room, and that the place was well supplied with London and local newspapers.

There was a small lending library, and a band played, while ladies and gentlemen conversed together, or simply stared. As today, windows overlooked King's Bath, where bathers, healthy and sick, waded and spluttered.

Seeing so many invalid bathers must have made Beau Nash realize the need for a hospital. Today, near the Tompion Clock is a statue of him with his hand resting on a plan of the Royal National Hospital for Rheumatic Diseases in Bath.

We now see that his rules on social etiquette had a lasting influence on the nation, for Bath drew together very diverse classes of society, each equally ignorant of the other. They were brought into daily contact, from the early bathing and breakfast to eleven p.m. when dancing ceased, on a footing of equality, all submitting to the same social discipline.

By Jane Austin's time the Pump Room had been enlarged, demolished and then rebuilt in 1795 as the Pump Room we know today. The main architect of the present exterior was Thomas Baldwin, and John Palmer was responsible for the interior.

In Victorian times Charles Dickens, describing the Pump Room in 'Pickwick Papers', wrote: 'There are baths near at hand in which a part of the company wash themselves, and a band plays afterwards to congratulate the remainder on their having done so!'

Nowadays balls are special occasions during winter months or perhaps the Bath Festival. Many still enjoy their daily coffee in the Pump Room reading newspapers or looking at the tourists who come from all parts of the world. The atmosphere is airy and tranquil with the small band playing light music.

Our age is supposed to be fast and noisy, so it is amusing to read about the Pump Room in Smollett's 'Humphrey Clinker' published 1771, his description 'The noise of music playing in the gallery; the heat and flavour of such a crowd, and the hum and buzz of their conversation gives one the headache next day. But afterwards, all things become familiar and even agreeable! '

Eighteenth century Georgians renting houses in Bath for the season enjoyed breakfast with friends and would have praised this delicious preserve.

*

APPLE JELLY MARMALADE

Ingredients: 4 lb cooking apples; 3-4 sweet oranges; juice of 1 large lemon; granulated sugar.

Wipe and quarter the apples and place in a preserving pan. Wipe and peel the oranges and, reserving the peel, cut the orange flesh up and add to the apples. Add the lemon juice and enough cold water to cover the apples. Bring up to the boil, then simmer for 1-1½ hours until very soft. Mash the fruit to a good pulp. Strain the pulp and juice through a scalded jelly bag.

Cut the white pith away from inside the reserved peel. Cut the peel into neat strips and then shred very finely. Put the shredded peel in a saucepan and add water to cover generously. Simmer gently, covered with a lid, until the peel is quite soft and tender — about 1½ hours. Then strain and reserve the peel.

Meanwhile measure the strained juice from the apples back into the preserving pan — there should be about 4 pints. Add 1 lb sugar for each 1 pint juice. Stir over low heat to dissolve the sugar, then boil briskly for 15 minutes, skimming well to clear the jelly. Add the cooked shredded peel and continue boiling for a set — about 5 minutes more. When a set is obtained draw off the heat. Cool for about 30 minutes, stir the jelly to distribute the peel evenly and pour into clean dry pots. Cover when hot and seal when cold. Makes about 8 lb.

* * *

Sheep farmers from the Mendips in Somerset provided Georgian Bath visitors with fresh meat. (Charterhouse monks first reared sheep on these hills about the 12th century.)

*

LAMB AND APPLE PIE

Serves 4.
4 oz flour and 2 oz butter made into short-crust pastry, or use 6 oz ready-made. Make the pastry and put it in a cool place to rest while the filling is prepared.
1 lb lean lamb or mutton without bone, or about 2 lb with bone; 8 oz cooking apples; 3 oz onions; salt and pepper.
Cut the meat in small pieces. Peel, core and slice the apples, skin and slice the onions. Put these into a 1 pt. pie dish in layers, seasoning well with salt and pepper. Add cold water to half fill the dish.
Roll the pastry and cover the pie in the usual way. Cut a slit in the top of the crust. Bake 450°F (gas 8) for 10 minutes, then 300°F (gas 2) for rest of time until the meat is tender (about 1½ hours). If the pastry browns before this, cover the top loosely with a piece of foil.
Serve the pie hot or cold.

* * *

Imagine a cast iron range blackened each morning by the housemaid ready for cook to prepare her culinary dishes. Baked apples would be tender in time for the main meal of the day served about 4 p.m.

*

BAKED APPLES

Ingredients: 1 large apple per portion. Water or cider to come ¼ in. up the sides of the apples; dates, raisins, nuts, chopped peel, mincemeat, and spices as optional flavourings for the stuffing; large and perfect cooking apples; 1 tbls sugar, honey, syrup or black treacle per apple; butter or magarine.

Wash the apples and remove the cores with an apple corer. Though they may be peeled they are best cooked with the skins on, but slit the skin in a circle about half-way down the sides of the apples. This prevents the skins from bursting during cooking. Place the apples in a shallow baking dish or individual dishes and fill the centres with sweetening and fruit or spices as desired. Put a knob of butter or magarine on top of each. Pour in the liquid and bake 400°F (gas 6) until they feel tender when pierced with a cooking fork or skewer. Baste occasionally during cooking. About 40-45 minutes.

Serve hot or cold with cream or custard.

* * *

This is a pudding for residents who return to their lodgings promptly at meal-time!

*

APPLE AND ORANGE WITH CARAMEL

If you want the caramel to remain in crunch pieces, add it just before serving.
Serves 4.
1 lb apples. Peel, core and quarter and place in cold water to keep them a good colour. ¼ pint water; 2 oz sugar.
Bring to the boil, stirring to dissolve the sugar. Add the apple, turning the pieces over in the syrup. Cover the pan and poach gently until just tender, turning the apple over occasionally. Remove from heat; leave to cool in the covered pan.
2 oz castor sugar.
Put in a small thick pan and heat, without stirring, to melt the sugar. Continue cooking until it forms a brown caramel. Pour this into a small oiled tin, about 6 in. diameter. Leave to set and become cold, then break it up into small pieces.
1 large or 2 small oranges. Peel the rind from a small orange or half a large one and cut the rind into fine shreds. Boil these in

water for 3 minutes. Cut the flesh of the oranges in small pieces. Add the rind and the flesh to the apples and sprinkle with the pieces of caramel.

* * *

'*A word fitly spoken is like apples of gold in pictures of silver.*' Proverbs XXV.II.

I WONDER IF THE MONK STILL CHANTS

I used to avoid Old Lilliput Lane in case I mysteriously disappeared within Sally Lunn's house! Built in 1482, it is the oldest house in Bath.
'I'd like to have you here all by yourself,' old Miss Mabel Byng-Johnson had said, smiling, when I visited the house with my husband and parents, and had asked too many questions about ghosts.
The tall, narrow house then belonged to Miss Byng-Johnson, who lived there alone. She used to open it to the public, taking them on conducted tours. The nervous would just peer in through the dusty paned window. The brave rang the bell, and were taken to the top of the house, from where they were guided through the surprisingly spacious floors down to the first sub-basement. Deeper cellars existed, and little did they imagine Miss Byng-Johnson was going to take them down steps into the bowels of Bath, where Roman prisoners were once taken through an archway to their fate, dragging their chains across the flagstones, according to the old lady. The archway is now bricked up, but Miss Johnson told us of a monk still chanting prayers at night for the prisoners.
'The monk was a good man,' said our guide, which was little comfort so far down beneath the house, with our young boxer dog sniffing round the cellar, my parents looking green, and my husband's hair actually standing on end!
Incredibly Miss Byng-Johnson then took us down to another cellar, where we saw stalactites and stalagmites and some human teeth. We were glad to start climbing the stairs again.
Higher, but still below street level, we entered Sally Lunn's stone-flagged kitchen. It was about 1680 that Sally Lunn lived here and baked her famous cakes, helped by a negro boy. With no daylight, he used to work all day in the hot kitchen, using long-handled scoops to pull cakes out from ovens built deep into thick walls.
How good it felt to enter the parlour with its beautifully polished

applewood floor and to admire the wide fireplace. With a low ceiling we thought how welcoming it must have been to ladies and dandies with the fire ablazing and the glow of candlelight, whilst outside wind whipped down the alley.

Now I stand outside this house and stare with delight. The dismal exterior has been transformed into a bright café. Window boxes enhance white-painted windows with red geraniums, pink and white petunias and sky blue lobelia spilling out in pretty confusion.

'Oh dear, the café is closed,' says a woman nearby to her friend, 'and we have come all this way.' We peer through the bow window. Everywhere looks airy and white with pine furniture and antique bric-a-brac. The two women standing beside me agree to come back another day.

I remember elderly Miss Byng-Johnson trying to reassure me by saying, although she knew the house had known many ghosts, all were at rest except the monk. Does he still chant, I wonder, and does he now have a companion? Not long after Miss Byng-Johnson showed her house to my family, I read she had died. For one who had known Sally Lunn's house so well, could her ghost be there, peacefully enjoying herself after the café is closed for the night.

Sally Lunn would have approved of the chic restaurants visitors today enjoy in Bath. Here is a chance to make your own Sally Lunn tea cakes from the old-fashioned recipe. It was in her time that William of Orange came to the throne. Try the 300 year old recipe, and Dutch apple cake.

*

SALLY LUNN TEA CAKES

Mix ½ a teaspoonful of salt in 1 lb of flour and add 3 tablespoons of sugar. Melt ½ oz of butter into ½ pint of milk. When milk is warm pour it over ½ oz of compressed yeast. Add a little well-beaten egg and a little grated nutmeg. Stir lightly into the

flour with a wooden spoon, cover with a cloth and set in a warm place to rise. Knead on a floured board, place in tins and allow to rise again. Bake in a hot oven for 15 to 20 minutes, 425°F (gas 7).
The tea cakes are usually 3 to 4 inches in diameter. They are best split in two then toasted and served with cream and jam.

* * *

This chutney is good with cold meats and a happy reminder if your marrow won a prize in the local horticultural show.

*

APPLE AND MARROW CHUTNEY

Cut 8 lbs of marrow into small cubes. Sprinkle with salt and leave overnight. Drain well. Peel and core 4 lbs of cooking apples and place in a large preserving pan with the marrow, 2 lbs of sliced onion, 3 lbs of sugar, 4 pints of vinegar, 1 teaspoonful of paprika, a little salt and 1 oz of pickling spices tied in muslin bag. Cook over a slow heat until it thickens and then pot.
When preparing the marrow remove the skin and pips.

* * *

This 300 year old recipe is translated for modern use and is named after Prince William of Orange who left his Dutch homeland in the late 17th century to become King William in this country with his English wife Queen Mary.

*

WILLIAM AND MARY PIE

Ingredients: 4 cooking apples, peeled and cored; 3-4 oz butter; 4 oz sugar; 4 egg whites; 8 oz puff pastry; grated lemon rind.
Method: Cook apples until soft. Add butter and sugar beaten together, and add grated lemon peel. Whip egg whites until stiff and fold into apple. Put into dish. Cover with puff pastry. Bake in a moderately hot oven, 400°F (gas 6) for 20-30 minutes. Serve warm with cream.

* * *

A typical recipe from the Netherlands to share with friends at a coffee get-together.

*

DUTCH APPLE CAKE

Serves 6.
6 oz self-raising flour; 1 level teaspoon baking powder; 3 oz castor sugar; 1 large egg; 6 tablespoons milk; 1 oz melted butter. For the topping: 1 oz melted butter; 1 lb cooking apples; 3 oz castor sugar; 1 level teaspoon cinnamon.
Sift the flour and baking powder into a bowl and add sugar. Mix together egg, milk and melted, but not hot, butter. Pour into the centre of the flour and, using a wooden spoon, beat the mixture gently, gradually drawing in the flour. Then beat thoroughly for a moment to make a smooth, fairly soft, mixture. Spoon the mixture into a small, well-buttered shallow baking tin, approximately 11 by 7 inches. Spread the mixture level, and prepare the topping.
Brush the top with the melted butter. Peel, core and thinly slice apples. Arrange the apples over the surface of the cake, laying them in overlapping rows for display. Mix together the castor sugar and cinnamon and then generously sprinkle the mixture over the apple slices. Place in the centre of a hot oven 400°F (gas 6) and bake for 35 minutes, or until the apples are tender and golden.
Cool, and cut in squares.

* * *

> *When Eve upon the first of Men*
> *The apple press'd with special cant,*
> *Oh! What a thousand pities then*
> *That Adam was not Adamant!*
>   Thomas Hood (1799-1845)

THE LINLEY FAMILY

Imagine on your way to the theatre on an early summer's evening in 1767, you probably passed beneath the Portico Arch into Pierrepont Place. It was then called Orchard Street. The Musical Linley family lived at No. 1 just a few doors away from the New Theatre. You probably heard Elizabeth Linley singing, for on a warm evening windows would be thrown open to catch the breeze.

Perhaps twelve year old Elizabeth Ann was practising with her brother Tom, eleven. Young as they were these children were to perform professionally at a concert in May. Elizabeth sang and Tom played the violin.

Their father, Mr. Thomas Linley, was perhaps in the music room at the back of the house, teaching a fee-paying pupil. Mrs. Linley, his wife, would be checking bills. She was known to keep a strict hold on the family's finances.

Spitalfield silk cost £4 a yard for Elizabeth's billowing concert dress, and Mr. Linley could be expected to wear shoes with silver buckles, costing over £20, with lace at his throat at least £40.

In those days he had to look like a gentleman, appearing to keep the high standards of his patrons. If someone had prophesied their future in your ear, you would have stood enchanted in front of the small Georgian house with its white doorway and ornamental pineapples, and maybe saddened too. Within four years the family became wealthy enough to move to Royal Crescent. In 1776 Mr. Linley was appointed musical director of Covent Garden in London. He was considered the finest singing teacher of his time.

Royalty and all society acclaimed Elizabeth for her brilliant singing and beauty.

Young Tom visited Italy and became friends with Mozart, who described the boy as a true genius.

Five other brothers and sisters were also musically gifted. Yet I mention sadness. Life in Linley House may have been the family's happiest time, for although Mr. and Mrs. Linley had short tempers, they had charming children.

Gainsborough, the artist, frequently painted Elizabeth and the family. Did he have the perception to realise the strain imposed on their delicate constitutions?

At that time it was usual for children to earn money for their parents, and I doubt Mr. Linley saw any danger pushing forward his young, growing family. Life often was brief.

Five daughters died before their fortieth birthday; only two of the seven sons lived to an old age. From the whole family only the two eldest daughters left descendants. One of them is Lord Snowdon. When Princess Margaret and Lord Snowdon decided to call their eldest son Lord Linley, perhaps they hoped he would be a musical child.

Recently I visited Linley House. Designed by John Wood, Bath's most famous architect, it was built in 1742 for plasterer John Hutchins. Now it has been used for some years as the headquarters of Bath Festival Society, being rescued from neglect by the Portico Trust organisation. Furnished with pictures on loan it is pleasant to stand in the small elegant rooms with fine plasterwork restored after the removal of layers of lime wash.

I pondered how Elizabeth Linley eloped with the playwright Richard Sheridan and that after her short lifetime giving so much pleasure with her singing, she is laid to rest in Wells Cathedral.

Whereas the public still enjoy performances of Sheridan's plays, it is Elizabeth's beauty that has been handed down for posterity through the brushwork of Gainsborough, the artist.

Apples would have been an important fruit in the Linley's diet, being plentiful and quite reasonable, both considerations taken into account by Mrs. Linley when housekeeping for her large family.

*

APPLE PURÉE

Wash cooking apples, wipe quarter and core. Rub ½ oz butter over sides and bottom of a large pan. Slice apples into pan. Add a strip of lemon rind. Cover with a greased paper and a lid, and cook gently until soft. Stir occasionally. Rub through sieve or strainer. Rinse out pan and return purée to it. Add sugar, 4 oz to a pint of purée. Cool rapidly stirring all the time. Bottle in hot jars. Useful for flans in winter.

APPLE PANCAKE

Ingredients: 2 eggs; 4 oz flour; ½ pt. milk; pinch of salt; sugar; apples.
Method: Make a pancake batter using egg yolks only — fold in beaten egg whites. Peel and core apples — slice into rounds. Heat fat in frying pan, pour batter into pan, place sliced apples on top. When brown on underside, turn pancake over and cook on other side — using a little more fat — until well cooked. Before serving hot, sprinkle with sugar. (Makes several pancakes.)

* * *

Good enough for the Linley family's Christmas dinner!

*

PRUNE STUFFING AND SPICED APPLES FOR ROAST GOOSE

Serves 8.
10 lb oven-ready goose; a little flour.
For the prune stuffing: ½ lb soaked prunes; liver from the goose; 6 oz fresh white breadcrumbs; ¼ level teaspoon powdered mace; salt and freshly milled pepper; 3 oz butter.
For the spiced apples: 6 apples; 4 oz sultanas; 4 oz soft brown sugar; 1 teaspoon mixed spice; 4 oz butter; few whole cloves.

Simmer the prunes in the liquid they soaked in for about 10 minutes until tender but not soft. Drain the prunes, remove the stones and rub the flesh through a sieve to make a purée. Cover the goose liver with cold water and bring up to the boil. Simmer for about 5 minutes, then drain. Chop finely and then pound to a paste. Using a fork, mix the prune purée, the liver paste, the breadcrumbs and mace together. Season with salt and pepper. Melt the butter over low heat, then, using a fork, stir into the stuffing. Pack the stuffing into the tail-end of the bird and skewer fasten.

While the bird is roasting, prepare the spiced apple. Wash and remove the cores from the apples, keeping the apples whole. Run the top of a sharp knife blade round the centre of each apple just to pierce the skin. This helps to prevent the apple skins from splitting during baking. Wash and chop the sultanas and mix in a bowl with the sugar and half the spice. Heat the butter in a saucepan until melted, then draw off the heat and stir in the remaining spice. Pour half the spiced butter into an ovenproof baking dish or small roasting tin. Place the apples in the tin and fill the centre of each one with the fruit and sugar mixture. Stick each apple with two cloves and then pour over the remaining spiced butter. About 40 minutes before the end of the cooking time for the goose, place the apples in the oven to bake along with the goose. Baste the apples occasionally with the butter in the dish. When the goose is ready, lift from the tin and remove any skewers.

Arrange on a serving dish and surround with the spiced apples and serve with a thin gravy.

* * *

Should Mrs. Linley be in good spirits a pudding to relish.

*

APPLE AND APRICOT FLAN

Quantities for a 7-8 in. flan:
Ingredients: 1 lb cooking apples; ½ tsp grated lemon rind; 2 tbls sugar; ½ oz butter; 1 tbs water; omit this if the apples are juicy.
Method: Use half the apples first. Peel, core and slice them and mix with the other ingredients. Stew to a thick pulp. Cool.
Short-crust pastry using 4 oz flour and 2 oz butter or use 6 oz ready-made. Roll thinly to line a flan ring or tin. Spread the cold apple pulp in the bottom.

Peel, core and slice the rest of the apples very thinly. Arrange them on the apple pulp in a spiral design. Sprinkle with sugar and bake 400°F (gas 6) until the pastry is firm, ½-¾ hr.

2 oz apricot jam (2 tbls); 1 tbls water. Heat together until syrup, sieving if necessary to make a smooth glaze. As soon as the flan comes out of the oven brush this glaze all over the apples. Cool the flan and then lift it on to a serving dish. Serve cold.

* * *

A was an apple-pie
B bit it;
C cut it.

Nursery rhyme.

THE THEATRE AT BATH

Today the Theatre Royal is attracting a new, younger audience to see well-rehearsed plays in refurbished surroundings. The old intimacy of the Theatre Royal continues to enchant and it is live theatre that the public will drive miles to see, escaping the boredom of television soapbox entertainment. Optimists have foretold it was just a question of time, before people became bored with T.V. programmes and staying indoors.

Two hundred years ago there was no such rival, and the theatre flourished. When the first Bath Theatre Royal was built in 1750 on a site called Orchard Street, it was known as the New Theatre near the home of the Linley family. In those early days it competed with a theatre belonging to a Mr. Simpson. That gentleman must have held much influence on theatre-goers, for the perfumed rich, and unwashed poor would sit together on benches in so small a theatre beneath a ballroom, that the architect Wood once described it as a cellar! When Mr. Simpson died in 1755 the Theatre Royal in Orchard Street had the monopoly of dramatic performances, and with John Palmer as theatrical manager, it became very popular.

George III granted the royal patient in 1768, Bath thereby having the first provincial theatre granted letters patient. The only 'Royal' theatres at that time were London's Drury Lane and Covent Garden.

Young Mrs. Sarah Siddons became famous in the Theatre Royal Bath, working hard to improve her technique. In later life she wrote: 'When I recollect all this labour of mind and body, I wonder I had strength and courage to support it, interrupted as I was by the cares of a mother, and by the childish sports of my little ones, who were often most unwillingly hushed to silence from interrupting their mother's studies.'

With this young family to support, she decided to leave Bath for London, and told her audience in a farewell speech that there were three reasons. To everyone's surprise Sarah Siddons produced her three small children on stage, addressing them with the words:

Stand forth, ye elves, and plead your mother's cause;
Ye little magnets, whose soft influence
Sends me adverturous on a larger main
In hopes that you may profit by my gain.

This was her benefit performance, and she appeared in 'The Distressed Mother'. We may smile at such obvious play on the audience's heart, but as she received £145. 18s that night, and a further £106. 13. for a similar farewell in Bristol, audiences must have admired her maternal sentiments as much as her exceptional qualities as an actress. At Drury Lane her family fortune was secured.

Actor Robert Elliston began a famous stage career at Bath in 1790. Fourteen years later, when he appeared in London, as soon as the doors were opened, the crush was so great, it was impossible to take the money. After his performance Elliston sent men round with pewter plates to collect entrance fees. The audience paid with satisfaction, and Elliston cleared £600. The Theatre Royal in Bath continued to flourish with Robert Elliston and Sarah Siddons returning to packed audiences.

In 1805 a larger theatre was built on the site of our present theatre in Bath's Beaufort Square. The Orchard Street building became a Roman Catholic Chapel and afterwards a Masonic Hall. For the early nineteenth century Theatre Royal over £5,000 was subscribed, the list of contributors headed by the Prince and Princess Charlotte of Wales and the Duke of York. Boxes were 5 shillings, the pit 3s and gallery 1s.6d. This theatre was spacious, elegant in crimson and gold and convenient with three lofty tiers supported by bronzed iron pillars to include private boxes, handsomely fitted with curtains, gilt rails and chairs.

In 1828 gas-lights were substituted for oil lamps as footlights. However, after the 1837 flu epidemic, when audiences stayed at home, the theatre began to struggle.

Not until 1847 was there a packed audience to listen to the renowned singer Jenny Lind.

Mr. James Chute became lessee the following year, and his enterprise brought fame back to the theatre...

However, on Good Friday in 1862 the Theatre Royal was destroyed by the biggest fire, Bath citizens had ever seen.

Remarkably the present Theatre Royal was completed by 1863. Ellen Terry made her first appearance in Bath on the first night as Titania in 'A Midsummer Night's Dream'.

Interior decorations depict this play and also 'Much Ado About Nothing', which was the last Shakespearean play acted in the old theatre before the fire.

Since the Theatre Royal was rebuilt in 1863, a ghost has become part of this theatre's tradition. During rehearsals an actress or actor sometimes sees a lady in grey walking round the lower circle to sit in the stage box. When asked who it is, the management has to admit no-one has been in the box, and that it must have been the reputed ghost, seen before wearing a grey habit.

She is a quiet lady, unlike the ghost next door in the Garrick's Head, who is prone to throw articles and stamp about. It seems two men had fought a duel in the lower lounge, which had been a gaming room belonging to Beau Nash. A woman had been the cause of the duel and tragically it was her lover, who was killed. The other man afterwards rushed upstairs to claim his prize, only to find she had hung herself on the door.

On the other side of the Theatre Royal's entrance is a Georgian building, where Beau Nash died as an old, impoverished man in 1762.

Many years afterwards, a tablet was erected in Bath Abbey to his memory. Outstanding functionary of his day, Nash was a pioneer in civic entertainment. Benevolent at heart, he spared no effort establishing the Bath Hospital, now of national importance in the treatment of rheumatic disease.

A refreshing lunchtime salad to enjoy before a matinée.

*

CARROT AND APPLE SALAD

Serves 4.

8 oz new carrots; 3 dessert apples; 4 tablespoons seedless raisins; 1 carton soured cream; 2 level teaspoons castor sugar; juice of ½ lemon.

Scrape the carrots and grate coarsely into a bowl. Peel, core and grate the apples and add with the raisins.

Mix together the soured cream, sugar and lemon juice and pour over the mixture. Toss with a fork to blend the ingredients and serve.

* * *

After a successful theatrical evening performance, a French treat.

*

JACQUES PANCAKES (These pancakes are a speciality of the country districts of Périgord.)

Ingredients: ¼ lb flour; 1 gill milk; 1 dessertspoon olive oil; a pinch of salt; 1 teaspoon sugar; ½ glass water; 2 eggs, 2 or 3 apples.
Method: Make a pancake batter with the flour, oil, salt, milk, water and eggs; beat it very well, then let it rest for several hours.
Peel the apples and cut them in very thin slices; sprinkle a little castor sugar over them and a squeeze of lemon juice. Heat a small, thick frying pan and coat with a thin film of oil or butter; drop in a tablespoon of the batter and let it spread out as much as possible; on top of the pancake place 2 slices of apple, cover them with a little more of the batter and turn the pancake over; let it cook a little longer than the ordinary pancake on account of the apples; the pancakes are served flat, sprinkled with sugar, and eaten quickly.
The apples can be soaked in a little rum or brandy should it be available.

* * *

In honour of the famous soprano Jenny Lind from Sweden.

*

SWEDISH APPLE SOUFFLÉ

Serves 4.
2 oz brown sugar (4 tbls); 4 tbls water.
Heat the sugar and water together in a pan until the sugar dissolves.
1½ lb apples. Peel, core and quarter and cook in the syrup until they are soft. Place them in a fireproof dish and leave to cool.
2 egg whites; 2 oz sugar; 2 tsp ground rice or semolina; 2 tbls ground almonds; almond essence.
Beat the egg whites until stiff. Fold in the other ingredients, adding almond essence to taste. Spread this over the apples and bake until lightly brown and set, about ½-¾ hr in oven 350°F (gas 4). Serve hot or cold with custard sauce or whipped cream.

* * *

To calm stage nerves on a chilly winter's night!

*

MULLED WINE (to serve hot)

1 dessert apple.
Wash the apple and bake it in a moderate oven for about 10 minutes to heat it through 375°F (gas 5).
A pinch of mixed spice; 2 tbls honey; 2 tbls sweet sherry; 1 bottle red wine.
Put in a pan and heat almost to boiling. Serve in a bowl with the apple floating on top. Use a ladle for filling the glasses, which should be warmed.

* * *

BATH ABBEY

Bath Abbey looks glorious in sunshine. Shoppers in town enjoy walking through Abbey Churchyard.
I pushed the heavy doors of the dark entrance, and then stood at the back of the Abbey gazing upwards to the fan vaulting, marvelling that man could chisel such beauty out of stone. I was reminded of a walk beneath huge trees in Bath's Victoria Park, where one looks up at the lofty branches meeting overhead; indeed a natural magnificence. To me, the fan vaulting of the Abbey has a similar quality, perfect for a house of God. The more frequent the visits, the deeper an appreciation of this Abbey, for its survival has often been in jeopardy.
In 603 A.D. Pope Gregory the Great appointed Augustine to lead a Roman mission to spread Christianity across England. By the end of the seventh century there was a small Celtic stone church in Bath, dedicated to St. Michael.
At the end of the eight century a Saxon Abbey stood eastward of our present Abbey, dedicated to St. Peter. Within two hundred years this had become one of the foremost churches in Saxon England.
However, when William the Conqueror died, barons in the West Country destroyed Bath and the church. In 1088 King Rufus sold the ruins of Bath and its Abbey for 500 pounds of silver to John de Villula, a native of Tours, who was chaplain and physician to the King. He was consecrated Bishop of Bath. Bishop John began to build an Abbey with his Norman trained architects and builders, that was so vast the present Abbey stands only upon the nave! Later damaged by fire, it was restored by the time St. John's Hospital was founded in 1180. More pilgrimages were made to Bath, bringing prosperity to the city.
A Benedictine Priory also developed Bath as a healing centre. However, by the fourteenth century this Priory was corrupt, and the church was ruined to its foundations.
In 1499, Bishop Oliver King rebuilt the smaller Abbey we know today. He fancied he heard a voice say: 'Let an Olive establish

the crown, and a King restore the church,' a pun on his name.
The following century after the dissolution of the monasteries, Bath Abbey suffered ruin again. By 1574, when Queen Elizabeth I visited Bath, she was so distressed to see the ruined Abbey she ordered collections throughout her kingdom for its restoration, and also St. John's Hospital. The Abbey became Bath's civic church.
Since, many alterations have been made, though not always good ones. In 1833 the beautiful wrought-iron communion rail was sold to William Beckford, who used it as a balcony rail for his house in Lansdown Place West. The Dowager Lady Noble rescued it in 1960, giving the rail back to the Abbey, where it is now used as a fine wrought-iron screen in the north transept.
On 19th May 1963 the Archbishop of Canterbury dedicated a modern silver cross and pair of candlesticks, which look beautiful against the rich carving of the sanctuary and stained glass east window.
Around the walls of the Abbey are tablets, reminders of family love in time of death. See their names and imagine how the Abbey bells once rang out joyfully in welcome, when many arrived in Bath as fashionable visitors nearly two hundred years ago. They would have taken up residence in Georgian houses you see today, and made a permanent home for their families in the city. Often they were retired admirals, colonels, men of the cloth, architects, builders, artists, writers and their ladies, not forgetting the nobility.
I agree with Henry William Watson, the naturalist, who said: 'I haunted Bath Abbey, and the more I saw of it, the more I loved it.'

Dishes fit to tempt a Bishop's palate!

*

BATH APPLE AND BACON CHARLOTTE

Ingredients: 8 oz bacon rashers; a little mustard; 3 large cooking apples, peeled and cored; 4 oz butter; 8 oz white breadcrumbs; 8 oz cheese, grated; pepper and salt.
Method: Chop the rashers, reserving 4 for topping. Place chopped rashers in a greased dish. Spread thinly with mustard. Grate the apples. Melt butter in a pan. Add crumbs, apple and 6 oz of the cheese. Put mixture on top of the bacon. Sprinkle with remaining cheese. Place 4 rashers on top.
Bake in oven 350°F (gas 4) for 45 minutes.

WELLS APPLE CHUTNEY

Ingredients: 2 lb apples; 1 lb onions; 1 lb soft brown sugar; ½ lb raisins; 1½ pts malt vinegar; 2 oz chopped walnuts; 2 oz mustard; 2 oz salt; 2 oz ginger; 1 tablespoon curry paste; 1 teaspoon cayenne pepper.
Method: Peel and chop apples and onions. Boil sugar and vinegar. Mix altogether and simmer for approximately 2 hours until thick. Pot.

APPLE AND BRANDY PUDDING (A country sweet from the Berry district of France.)

Peel and slice a pound of apples, and put them in a dish with a little sugar and 2 tablespoons of brandy.
Make a batter with ½ lb of flour, 2 eggs, a pinch of salt, 3 tablespoons of sugar and a tumbler of milk.
Stir the apples into the batter and pour it into a shallow buttered tin and cook for 45 minutes in a moderate oven, 350°F (gas 4).

MARY'S GLASTONBURY APPLE CAKE

Ingredients: 4 oz self-raising flour; 3 oz castor sugar; 2 oz butter; 1 or 2 eggs (mixture should be moist but not wet); 1 lb apples (peeled and cut); 1 level teaspoon cinnamon; 1 tablespoon soft brown sugar.

Method: Sift flour with a pinch of salt. Cream sugar and butter then beat in egg. Add flour and stir in prepared apples. If necessary, add a little milk. Put into a greased cake tin or fireproof dish and bake in a moderate oven 350-375°F (gas 4-5) for 45 minutes or until nicely browned. Mix cinnamon with soft brown sugar and sprinkle over top. Cut into slices and serve hot or cold with custard sauce or cream.

* * *

Keep me as the apple of an eye,
hide me under the shadow of thy wings.
Ib. XVII. 8 Book of Common Prayer.

THE GUILDHALL

The Guildhall in Bath is an important building to me; a perpetual symbol of local government, about which I might disagree sometimes, but value as essential to a democratic way of life.
Thomas Baldwin, the City architect, redesigned the old seventeenth century building in 1775 and built the Guildhall's magnificent Banqueting Room. Wings were added in 1893.
During a General Election in the 1960's I entered the Guildhall to help scrutinise the vote count. Even the sparkling beauty of the Banqueting Room chandeliers hardly tempted a glance from heads bent over piles of votes. One touch of political gaiety was the Liberal Agent's tangerine hat; a morale-booster for any losing Liberal candidate! At last the results were ready. Downstairs went the victorious candidate, followed by a gallant loser, both to be hailed with cheers from supporters wedged tight in the entrance hall, a place sporting masses of colour with banks of potted hydraneas. In the dark night outside the Guildhall, a crowd waited to hear short speeches, which they received with cheers or laughter. Such good spirits would not have seemed out of place in the middle ages when British democracy took root.
Another time visiting the Guildhall, I viewed an exhibition of Ancient Charters. 'Elizabeth I must have been a far-sighted woman,' said my guide as we were looking at her beautifully illuminated Charter giving the City of Bath powers to appoint a recorder and other officers, to organise affairs of the City themselves.
Queen Elizabeth I's Charter meant a big step forward in democratic local government since the fourteenth century, when King Edward III's Charter to Bath first allowed citizens to appoint their own 'taxers' and clerks to assess levy taxes.
Also on exhibition were corporation accounts, a special one being made out to William Parker and Company, Fleet Street, London for £266.10.9d., the sum paid for the impressive chandeliers hanging in the Banqueting Room and dated 15th May 1778. I admired silver plate, rarely on view, a superb piece being the

silver gilt Prince of Wales Grace Cup and Salver. It seems in October 1738 Frederick, Prince of Wales, and the Princess of Wales had been so pleased with their Bath visit that before leaving the Prince cleared the prison of all debtors and presented 1,000 guineas towards the General Hospital. The following year he gave the Cup and Salver, which were brought from London by Beau Nash.

Shakespeare refers to the crab apple drink of great antiquity 'Lambs Wool' when Puck in Midsummer Night's Dream says:

> And sometime lurk I in a gossips bowl,
> In very likeness of a roasted crab,
> And when she drinks, against her lips I bob.

*

LAMB'S WOOL, known probably to Queen Elizabeth I

A warming, cheerful drink made from 2 pints strong hot ale; 1 lb pulp of roasted apples; 3 teaspoons mixed spice; a little sugar; 1 or 2 eggs beaten up in thin cream and nowadays enough whisky to counteract the fatness of the cream.
Mix together and drink with quietness of content!

APPLE AND HORSERADISH SAUCE (for cold meat, poultry or fish)

Serves 4.
½ tsp dry mustard; 1 tsp water. Combine to make a smooth paste.
2 medium-sized apples, or 1 apple and 1 medium-sized carrot; 2 tbs lemon juice.

Peel the apple and carrot and grate finely, mixing at once with the lemon juice. Mix in the mustard. 1 tsp sugar; 2 tbls grated horseradish.
Add and mix well.

PORCUPINE APPLES

Ingredients: 3 large apples; 2½ cups of water; quarter cup of sugar; 2 tablespoons lemon juice, flaked almonds.
Method: Peel the apples, cut in half and remove core. Bring the water, sugar and lemon juice to the boil in a large shallow pan. Add the apples and simmer, cover until tender turning the pieces once. Arrange apple halves, cut side down, on a deep serving dish. Boil the syrup in which the apples were cooked until it is reduced to 2 cups.
Meanwhile spike almonds into apples. Pour on syrup, cool and chill. Serve with cream or custard sauce.

WEST COUNTRY APPLE CAKE

Ingredients: 1 cooking apple (about ¼ lb); half a lemon; 8 oz self-raising flour; pinch of salt; 4 oz butter; 4 oz soft brown sugar; ¼ pt milk; 1 large egg.
Icing: 8 oz icing sugar; 2 teaspoons lemon juice.
Method: Peel, core and chop apple. Grate the rind of the half lemon and squeeze the juice. Mix rind and juice with apple. Sift flour and salt together, and rub in butter, then stir in brown sugar. Beat egg and milk together and stir into mixture with the chopped apple. Grease a tin 7″ x 11″ x 1″ deep. Turn mixture into tin and spread evenly. Bake at 375°F (gas 5) for about 45 minutes.
Mix sifted icing sugar with lemon juice and enough water to make a thick spreading consistency. Pour onto cake while still warm and spread evenly. Cut into 16 slices when cold.

* * *

Stay me with flagons,
Comfort me with apples:
For I am sick of love.

Song of Solomon.

JANE AUSTEN IN BATH

Bath's historical background abounds with match-making! Jane Austen wrote in het novel 'Northanger Abbey' of Isabella Thorpe:

> *False and frivolous, eager to attract attention, bent on the conquest of a wealthy suitor and finding a favourable field for her manoeuvres in the Pump Room and Assembly Rooms.*

The city Jane Austen knew in 1800 is described in another novel 'Persuasion'. She wrote:

> *When Lady Russell was entering Bath on a wet afternoon and driving through the long course of streets from the Old Bridge to Camden Place, amidst the dash of other carriages and heavy rumble of carts and drays, the bawling of newsmen, muffin men, milkmen and ceaseless clink of pattens, she made no complaint. No, these were the noises that belonged to the Winter pleasures of Bath.*

In Jane Austen's day, most Georgian houses were let to visitors for about three months. It must have been enjoyable seeing new faces, and being caught up in the social whirl.
On 17th May 1799, Jane wrote to her sister Cassandra from 13, Queen Square:

> *We are exceedingly pleased with the house, the rooms are quite as large as we expected. Mrs. Bromley* (landlady) *is a fat woman in mourning, and a little black kitten runs about the staircase. When we first came, all the umbrellas were up, but now the pavements are getting very white again. My mother does not seem at all the worse for her journey, nor any of us, I hope, though Edward* (brother) *seemed rather fagged last night, and not very brisk this morning. But I*

> trust the bustle of sending for tea, coffee and sugar etc. and going out to taste a cheese himself, will do him good.
> There was a very long list of arrivals here in the newspaper yesterday, so that we need not immediately dread absolute solitude, and there is a public breakfast in Sydney Gardens every morning, so that we shall not be wholly starved. I am rather impatient to know the fate of my best gown, but I suppose it will be some days before Francis (another brother) can get through the trunk.

Jane Austen's trunk was too heavy to be included in her coach, when they travelled to Bath, and it was too heavy for several coaches afterwards!

Shopping was not such a success. On 19th June 1799, she wrote to Cassandra:

> I had no difficulty in getting a muslin veil for half a guinea, and not much more in discovering afterwards that the muslin was thick, dirty and ragged. I changed it consequently as soon as I could and considering what a state of imprudence had reduced me to, I thought myself lucky in getting a black lace one for sixteen shillings.

She also tried to buy artificial fruit, then in fashion, for her sister's hat, and was most concerned not to be overcharged. Jane wrote:

> We have been to the cheap shop near Walcot Church, but there are only flowers made there, no fruit. And as I could get four or five pretty sprigs of flowers for the same money which would buy one plum, I cannot decide, until I hear from you again.

Perhaps to lessen her sister's disappointment, she added:

> Besides I cannot help thinking it is more natural to have flowers grow out of the head than fruit!

Jane Austen enjoyed staying in Bath so much that the following January she wrote to her sister of the difficulty of both staying at the same time with their aunt in the Paragon. She admitted she did not want to be left behind, though two cost more to feed than one. To assist the housekeeping budget Jane promised to eat no Bath buns, of which she was most partial.
She also wrote:

> *My father and mother, wisely aware of the difficulty of finding in all Bath such a bed as their own, have resolved on taking it with them!*

Jane Austen was a fair minded girl, for she wrote another time:

> *We were visited by Mrs. and Miss Holder. It is the fashion to think them both very detestable, but they are so civil, and their gowns so white and nice, that I cannot utterly abhor them!*

In that letter to her sister Cassandra she continued:

> *Our grand walk to Weston* (village near Bath) *was again fixed for yesterday. Everyone of the party declined it under some pretence or other, except Mrs. Chamberlayne and myself. After the first two yards, half the inhabitants of Bath set off with us. It would have amused you to see our progress. We went up Sion Hill and returned across the fields. In climbing a hill, Mrs. C is very capital; I could with difficulty keep up with her, yet I would not flinch for the world.*

Such were the light-hearted days of Jane Austen in her twenties, during visits to Bath. I must not omit her fondness for dances, though they did not always come up to expectations.
During the summer of 1801 she wrote to Cassandra:

> *By 9 o'clock my uncle, aunt and I entered the Upper*

Assembly Rooms, and linked Miss Winstone with us. Before tea, it was rather a dull affair, but then the 'Before Tea' did not last long, for there was only one dance, danced by four couples. Think of four couples, surrounded by about a hundred people, dancing in the Assembly Rooms at Bath. After tea we cheered, for the breaking up of private parties sent some scores more to the Ball.

Jane Austen was born on 16th December 1775 at the Parsonage House of Steventon in Hampshire. Her father was a scholarly country vicar and her mother the former Miss Cassandra Leigh, daughter of another well-educated clergyman.

Jane had five brothers, two of whom became admirals in the British Navy, and her elder sister Cassandra. Never marrying herself, Jane Austen became the favourite aunt of her nephews and nieces. She was described by a nephew, writing his memoir of her, as 'not so regularly handsome as Cassandra, but rather tall, slender, animated and very attractive'.

Preferring to be anonymous, none of her novels appeared originally under her name. Yet, recognition came from an unexpected quarter. The dissolute Prince Regent made it known he would accept a dedication. This he duly received in Emma, though Jane Austen disapproved of his character, writing in a letter she 'hated him' for the treatment of the Princess.

Jane Austen appreciated her food and would recommend a young mistress show her cook the art of making light pastry for apple pie. It is said sifting the flour and quick handling with cold fingers is the secret of good pastry.

*

APPLE DOUBLE-CRUST PIE

6 oz flour and 4 oz butter made into short-crust pastry, or use 10-12 oz ready-made for 8 in. tart.

Use a flan ring or pie plate. Divide the pastry into two pieces, one a little bigger than the other. Use the larger piece for the bottom and the smaller for the top.

1 lb apples, cooking or dessert; 1 tsp grated lemon rind; tsp grated nutmeg or ground cinnamon; 2 tsp lemon juice; pinch of salt; 4-6 oz sugar.

Peel and core the apples and slice fairly thinly. Put apples, flavourings and sugar on the pastry. Cover with pastry, sealing the edges carefully. Cut small slits all over the top.

Place the tart on a baking tin in case juice boils over and bake until the pastry is lightly browned and the fruit cooked, shown by juice appearing in the slits in the top for 30 minutes 400°F (gas 7).

Serve the tart hot or cold, sprinkled with sugar, with cream or custard separately.

PORK FILLET WITH CIDER

Serves 4.

Ingredients: 1¼ lb pork tenderloin; 2 oz butter; 4 oz onions, skinned and chopped; 2 large eating apples; 6 oz long grain rice; 2 level teaspoons dried tarragon; ¾ pt. dry cider; ¼ pt. light stock; 2 level tablespoons French mustard; salt and milled pepper; 3 oz mixed nuts and raisins.

Method: Trim the pork fillet and slice diagonally into ½ in. pieces. Using a shallow, flameproof casserole, brown pork well in the heated butter, take out using a draining spoon.

Fry the chopped onion and apple in the residual butter for 5 minutes. Stir in the rice with the herbs, cider, stock, mustard and seasoning. Bring to the boil and stir in the chopped nuts and raisins. Place the pork on top of the rice in slightly overlapping lines. Cover the dish tightly.

Bake in the oven at 325°F (gas 3) for about 40 minutes or until the meat and rice are tender and most of the liquid absorbed.

JAMAICAN APPLES WITH RUM (another version of baked apples)

Stuff the apples with apricot jam and sprinkle chopped almonds on top. Use brown sugar for the sweetening and for the liquid half rum and half water. Baste with the liquid during cooking and serve hot with cream.

ELDERBERRY AND APPLE JELLY

Ingredients: Equal weight of elderberries and apples.
Method: Cut elderberries off sprays with scissors, leaving the short pieces of stalks for speed. Boil elderberries and apples separately in enough water to prevent burning. Strain and use 1 lb sugar to each pint of juice. Boil together until setting is indicated.
This is a delicious jelly, easily made.

* * *

*An apple a day
keeps the doctor away.*

Old saying.

ASSEMBLY ROOMS AND YEHUDI MENUHIN

'What gorgeous chandeliers... I've seen them on television, but this is fairyland! '
'Accoustics are not so good, I believe,' rejoined her companion.
With a host of music lovers we were entering the Assembly Rooms to listen to Yehudi Menuhin and the Festival Orchestra with Clifford Curzon, pianist. Seated, I looked around noticing not flowing hippy hair, instead neat coiffeurs, mostly of white and grey, for this was predominantly a middle-aged audience, whose taste in life was quality, possibly symbolised by a woman's diamond and jade ear-rings.
Musicians took their places, the men in white tie and tails, the women in long black dresses. As they tuned their instruments all empty seats suddenly filled. Lights dimmed, tuning ceased, and together we waited. Then with a wink from youthful Margaret Major, viola soloist, and a pause, Yehudi Menuhin appeared to welcoming applause. The orchestra, alert to his eye, began to play with Mr. Menuhin, the violin soloist. Soft, muted sounds flowed into the Assembly Room, with its gilt mirrors reflecting violinists as they swayed over their instruments, absorbed in Vivaldi's Concerto Funebre. Too soon the music died, like a rose in a summer shower. While the musicians retired briefly, a piano was brought to the centre, and Clifford Curzon appeared to his Bath audience. He is constantly in demand in America and on the Continent; I soon knew why. As well as being a superb musician, he reminded me of Mr. Pickwick in appearance, and (dare I say) in the enthusiasm and enjoyment he revealed in playing Mozart's Piano Concerto in B flat.
During the interval I saw a strangely familiar face. Not the Greek princess attending this concert, but a younger version of a white-haired friend of mine. We introduced ourselves, and indeed she was the daughter! She told me how Mr. Menuhin used to visit her school in Bath, when she was younger, and this particular evening she had arrived early, off-duty from nursing, hoping for a ticket.

She was in luck, and cheerfully spent her nursing prize money to attend the concert.

We quenched our thirst with cider, much to the amusement of the barman, and returned to the final part of the concert, Dvorak's Serenade for Strings in E.

My programme described the Serenade as the work of a young man, happily married, not yet saddened by the early death of his eldest child. Five times Yehudi Menuhin was recalled and the last movement was repeated as an encore, each one of us cherishing each beautiful sound in an evening of enrichment and peace.

Mr. Yehudi Menuhin, being a musician known internationally, might well enjoy these recipes, when travelling abroad.

*

WALDORF SALAD

Serves 4.

Ingredients: 4 firm dessert apples; 3 stalks celery; 1½-2 oz shelled walnuts; 2 tablespoons mayonnaise; 2 tablespoons lightly whipped cream; squeeze of lemon juice.

Method: Wipe the apples and leave on the peel if it is a pretty colour. Quarter and core the apples and cut into neat dice. Shred the celery and coarsely chop the walnuts.

Mix together the mayonnaise and lightly whipped cream to make a light dressing and sharpen with a squeeze of lemon juice. Combine at once with the prepared apples. Mix in the shredded celery and leave in a cool place until ready to serve. Just before serving, mix in the coarsely chopped walnuts.

NUSSKUCHEN

Ingredients: 4 oz butter; 4 oz castor sugar; 2 large eggs; 1½ oz ground hazelnuts or almonds; 1 teaspoon instant coffee; 1 tablespoon warm milk; 4 oz self-raising flour; pinch of salt.
For filling: 1 lb apples – peeled, cored and sliced; 2 tablespoons apricot jam, grated rind and juice of ½ lemon.
To decorate: Icing sugar (for dusting).
Method: Grease and flour 8" sandwich tin; set oven at 375°F (gas 5). Soften the butter in a bowl, add the sugar and work until light and fluffy. Separate the eggs and beat the yolks into the butter and sugar. Stir in the prepared nuts. Dissolve the coffee in the warm milk; sift the flour with the salt and whisk the egg whites until stiff. Fold the flour into the mixture with the coffee flavoured milk, then fold in the egg whites. Turn mixture into the prepared tin and bake in pre-set oven for about 25 minutes until the cake is firm to the touch and has shrunk slightly from the sides of the tin. Turn on to a rack to cool.
Meanwhile peel, core and slice the apples and place in a shallow pan with the jam, lemon rind and juice. Cover and cook until apples are soft; leave to cool.
Split the cake in half and fill with the cooled apple mixture. Finish with a dusting of icing sugar.

APPLE STRUDEL

Serves 4-6.
4 oz plain flour; pinch salt; 1 small egg; 2 tablespoons warm water; 2 teaspoons oil; 1½ oz melted butter.
For the filling: 1 lb cooking apples; 2 oz walnuts; 2 oz sultanas; 2-3 oz soft brown sugar; ¼ level teaspoon cinnamon or mixed spice; icing sugar.
Sift the flour and salt into a mixing basin and make a well in the centre. Mix together the egg, water and oil and pour into the centre of the flour. Mix to a soft dough, then turn out on to a clean working surface and work as for bread dought until the dough is smooth and elastic. Place the dough in a small basin, cover with a cloth and leave to rest for 30 minutes while preparing the filling.
Peel, core and slice the apples and coarsely chop the walnuts. Mix with the sultanas, sugar and cinnamon or mixed spice. Roll out the strudel dough to an oblong shape and lift on to a clean tea cloth. Using the floured backs of the hands and knuckles,

and working from the underside, pull and stretch the pastry gently in all directions. Keep the pastry spread out during work. When the pastry is ready it should be almost the size of a tea cloth and thin enough to see the pattern through. Brush generously with the melted butter and scatter the filling over the surface making a fairly generous layer of filling on the edge nearest to you.

Pick up the two nearest corners of the cloth and roll the strudel away from you. When rolled up flatten the two ends and trim away the edges. Roll over on to a greased baking tray and curl into a horseshoe shape. Brush all over with melted butter. Place in the centre of a hot oven 400°F (gas 6) and bake for the first 20 minutes, then reduce the heat to 375°F (gas 5) and bake for a further 10-15 minutes until the sides feel crisp. Dust with icing sugar. Run a palette knife under the strudel and lift on to a serving dish.

Serve hot or cold with cream.

ENGLISH APPLE SAUCE FOR ROAST PORK

Serves 4-6.
1 lb cooking apples; 2 oz sugar.
Peel, core and slice the apples and cook them in a saucepan with just enough water to prevent burning. Cook to a pulp. If a smooth sauce is wanted, rub the pulp through a sieve or put it in the electric blender. Add the sugar and reheat. Serve hot.

* * *

There is an old saying that when it rains on St. Swithin's Day, it is the Saint christening the apples.

3p SHOES SHINE IN MUSEUM OF COSTUME

'Do let me take you to the Museum of Costume at the Assembly Rooms,' I say to our visiting friends and relations. Why? I just cannot see it enough! This Museum has the largest and most detailed display of costume in the world. Here you can study exquisite embroidery on gentlemen's coats and waistcoats, as well as lovely detail of ladies clothing, remembering it was often special outfits like court clothes that families have treasured for years before donating or loaning them to the Museum of Costume, to be displayed with such elegance.

Mrs. Doris Langley Moore is the founder. Through her efforts you can see a green brocade hooped gown much the same as young Elizabeth Linley would have worn for an important concert. Childrens' clothes little differed years ago from adults' attire.

I have seen models of two ladies in white lawn dresses, such as Jane Austin and her sister Cassandra wore, aspiring to look like nymphs as was the fashion when they were young in 1800. There are beautiful baby clothes dating from the seventeenth century, which make you sigh at the poignant thought so many infants died within a year.

Perhaps the most exciting feature of the Museum are the period scenes, devised to show us how great-great grandmama spent her days, whether visiting the Draper's Shop, entertaining the family at home in the Drawing Room or taking a stroll in Bath during Victorian times. In the Underwear Room, corsets that women have worn during the past two hundred years make you smile, and you positively laugh at the bloomers.

I have a personal interest in this Museum of Costume, for by strange chance a pair of shoes once belonging to my mother-in-law are now given pride of place. Imagine a little girl, eight years old, taking her grandmother to see this Museum for the first time. 'Granny, look at those shoes with straps and pointed toes.' 'Good gracious Mandy, they are just like the pair I gave your mother for a jumble sale here in Bath.' 'Granny, they are your

shoes! I bought them back for 3d and then offered them to the Museum. I have a lovely letter addressed especially to me thanking me for giving the shoes.' My mother-in-law looked closely at the shoes of navy blue suede and leather vintage 1920's, and she remembered it was because they were too tight she hardly wore them, but kept them in a box for years! 'Well I never! To think I bought them in Swansea all those years ago, and now they are in this beautiful Museum of Costume.'
Perhaps all the shoes displayed were once too tight!

The Museum of Costume is quite breathe-taking with the silks and satins and embroidery. Ladies, once so tightly corsetted, must have just tasted a little of this and a little of that! So, here are recipes to tempt the palate.

*

APPLE AVOCADO SPECIAL

Serves 4.
Ingredients: 4 red dessert apples; 1 avocado pear; juice of 2 lemons; 2 oz mixed salted nuts; bunch watercress.
Dressing: ¼ level teaspoon each salt and pepper; 1 teaspoon sugar; 2 tablespoons salad oil.
Method: Core red dessert apples but do not peel, cut into thin slices. Slice avocado in half, remove stone, peel and cut into thin slices. Cover apple and avocado slices with lemon juice in small bowl to preserve colour. Just before serving drain and keep lemon juice for dressing. Add salted nuts to apple and avocado, toss in prepared dressing, arrange on dish and garnish with washed watercress. Serve with cold chicken or meats.
To make dressing: Mix salt, pepper and sugar with salad oil in small bowl, beat in lemon juice drained from apple and avocado, until well blended.

APPLE, ORANGE AND NUT FRUIT SALAD

Prepare 3-4 hrs in advance to allow flavours to blend together. Serves 4.
½ pt water, or half cider and half water; 2 tbls honey.
Bring to boil. Cool the syrup before adding the honey.
1 lb mixture apples with chopped dates & nuts; lemon juice and oranges.
Prepare the fruit and slice or chop in small pieces. Add to the syrup. It is a good idea to drop the fruit straight into the syrup as it is prepared. This will help to preserve the colour of fruits like apples.
Add 1-2 tbs liqueur for additional flavour and almonds for texture contrast.

APPLE AND WALNUT LOAF

Ingredients: 4 oz margarine; 4 oz castor sugar; 2 eggs; 1 tablespoon golden syrup or honey; 4 oz sultanas; 2 oz walnuts (chopped); 8 oz self-raising flour; pinch of salt; 1 level teaspoon mixed spice; 1 cooking apple, chopped.
Method: Put all ingredients into a bowl and mix for 2 minutes. Turn into greased loaf tin. Bake at 350°F (gas 4) for 1 hour then reduce heat for further 20 minutes.

APPLE CHEESE CRUMBLE

Serves 4.
2 oz grated Cheddar cheese; 1 lb cooking apples.
Peel and slice the apples. Put apples and cheese in layers in a 1½ pt baking dish or pie dish.
3 oz plain flour; ½ tsp ground cinnamon; 3 oz brown sugar; pinch of grated nutmeg. Mix in a bowl.
2 oz butter or margarine. Rub into the dry ingredients. Sprinkle over the fruit and cheese and bake until the apples are tender 375°F (gas 5). Serve hot or warm.

* * *

An apple tart without some cheese
Is like a kiss without a squeeze!

North Country Quotation.

WINTER WONDERLAND IN SYDNEY GARDENS

The Holborne Museum by Sydney Gardens is well worth a visit, especially if you have enjoyed the Victoria and Albert Museum in London. It is a miniature version, beautifully decorated and an elegant setting for silver, porcelain, pottery and paintings.
'Portrait of a Lady' is a favourite of mine, by Thomas Gainsborough who lived at 24 The Circus in Bath. Somehow he captured the fleeting expression of interest in her eyes and the humour of her smile. It is a pleasure to admire the fine detail of the blue silk dress, trimmed with white lace, and her fair complexion.
After your visit to the Holborne Museum you might like to enter the nearby Sydney Gardens. It happened to be a very cold morning when I visited these gardens for the first time. Even on such a freezing day I discovered a magial quality about Sydney Gardens, which had been laid out in 1795. It seemed a timeless place as I mounted a pleasing wrought-iron bridge to take a better look down the railway, which shot like a bolt beneath numerous small bridges. I doubt the Ministry of Transport had been here, for a notice on the bridge stated it was still the property of the Great Western Railway.
Disappointed no train came by, I decided to walk up the path to yet another wrought-iron bridge. This time I looked down to the Kennet and Avon Canal. A tiny waterfall splashed into the canal, where two swans were entwined in one another, oblivious to the cold. I felt an intruder upon their solitude, and sensed hostility from the larger swan's beady eye. Silently I passed over the bridge, away. Trees were bare still, yet there were everygreen shrubs between winding paths to give the gardens shape and beauty. Short pointed leaves of irises massed together promising spring. I stood at the highest point in Sydney Gardens and looked across the bridges below.
How many other gardens possess Regency charm together with a Victorian railway decorously dipped out of sight. Few indeed. It was also ghostly. When a woman in a voluminous red coat came

along a path leading a small dog, for a fleeting moment I imagined her from the past.

It is true Joseph Haydn conducted his lively music in Sydney Gardens while the audience in rich clothes watched a marionette performance. Bright coloured lanterns hung from trees and were lit at nightfall. Jane Austen recalled how she enjoyed watching firework displays in the gardens. I was just thinking of Haydn's Surprise Symphony composed to startle a peacefully nodding audience, when a train roared through the embankment, out of view. That startled me into reality!

Then I strolled into a summerhouse, and there on the stone walls were murals of Victorian hey-days, including a train with Rocket engine and open carriages with ladies in crinolines and the men in toppers. I laughed. Two gardeners passing by, looked at me curiously, so I quickly quit the pillared entrance and went down the pathways to the exit.

Walking back along Putterey Street in search of a café, I thought Sydney Gardens that morning were almost magical.

We know from Jane Austen's letters to her sister Cassandra that she visited Sydney Gardens, where refreshments were served. Composer Joseph Haydn would surely have been tempted to eat a tasty pie, after conducting one of his concerts in the Gardens.

*

PORK AND APPLE PIE

1½ pt pie dish; 1¼ lb fillet of pork, or other lean pork without bone; pinch of ground nutmeg; 1 tsp salt; pinch of pepper.
Cut the pork in thin slices and sprinkle it with the seasonings.
1 lb apples. Peel, core and slice and put them in the pie dish in layers with the meat, piling it up in the centre.
1 tsp brown sugar; 1 oz butter; ¼ pt white wine or cider. Add

sugar and wine to the pie and dot the top with small pieces of the butter.
8 oz puff pastry. Cover the pie in the usual way. Bake until the meat is tender 450°F (gas 8) for 10 minutes then 325°F (gas 3) for about 1¾ hrs.

APPLE CHARLOTTE

Serves 4.
4 oz fresh white breadcrumbs; 1½ oz castor sugar; 2 oz shredded suet.
For the apple mixture: 1 lb cooking apples; ½ oz butter; 1 tablespoon water; 2 oz soft brown sugar; 1 teaspoon golden syrup; rind of 1 lemon.
For the topping: 1 tablespoon Demerara sugar; ½ oz castor sugar.
Measure the breadcrumbs, castor sugar and suet into a small basin and set aside. Peel, core and slice the apples into a saucepan. Add the butter and water and place over low heat. Cover with a lid and stew gently until the apples are soft. Beat in the sugar, syrup and lemon rind and draw off the heat.
Well butter a 1½ or 2 pint baking dish. Place two-thirds of the crumb mixture in the dish and press over the base and sides of the dish. Pour in the apple mixture and top with the remaining crumb mixture. Sprinkle with the Demerara sugar and dot with the butter, cut into small pieces. Place in the centre of a moderately hot oven 375°F (gas 5) and bake for about 45 minutes to 1 hour until crisp and golden brown.
Serve hot.

APPLE SNOWBALLS

Ingredients: 4 apples; 4 cloves; whites of 2 eggs; 1½-2 tablespoons castor sugar; angelica.
Method: Peel and core apples. Place apples in pie dish with a clove in the centre of each. Pour in a little water and bake until apples are soft but not broken, in a medium oven about 30 minutes, 350°F (gas 4). Remove carefully into a shallow dish and arrange at equal distances apart. Whisk the egg whites until stiff, lightly fold in the castor sugar. Cover each apple all over with the meringue mixture and return to a cool oven, until set. Garnish with angelica and serve cold.

SURPRISE APPLE FLAMBÉ

Serves 4.
4 oz sugar; ½ pt water.
Heat in a saucepan large enough to take four apples in one layer, stir until the sugar dissolves and bring the syrup to the boil.
4 medium-sized apples; vanilla essence.
Peel and core the apples, using an apple corer. Add vanilla to the syrup to taste and poach the apples in this, turning them frequently until they are tender but not broken, about 30 minutes. Lift them on to a heat resistant serving dish. Keep hot. Boil the syrup rapidly to reduce and thicken it. Pour over the apples to give them a glaze, but there must not be a lot of syrup or it will douse the flame when the rum is ignited. Keep apples hot until ready to serve.
4 tbls warm rum.
Ignite, pour over the apples and serve while they are still flaming; specially attractive when served in individual heat resistant dishes.
Hand cream separately.

* * *

The friendly cow, all red and white
I love with all my heart.
She gives me cream with all her might
To eat with apple tart.
from 'The Cow' by Robert Louis Stevenson (1850-1894)

ORATORY IN THE ROMAN BATHS

Water, water everywhere! Today, pouring down from the skies as well as springing up 6,000 feet from below the surface. No wonder this city is called Bath.
Leaving the bustle of shoppers and their umbrellas I disappeared into the entrance of the Roman Baths. There awaited a surprise, for a retired actor had become a guide, and soon visitors and I were taken around on a tour. We enjoyed his eloquence, ignoring the chilled air while standing by the open King's Bath in cold November, and watched steam rise from the surface, while faint strains of a violin floated through the vapour, coming from the nearby Pump Room. Our guide told us Bath is one of four places in the world, where thermal springs rise; the others being in the Dolomites, Iceland and Colorado.
In Bath, the Romans built a reservoir over the hot spring, which is 120°F and this pumped water to the mineral hospital, as well as supplying constant hot water to the swimming baths. Spring water emptying from the Great Roman Bath still flows through the 6 ft. high Roman drain to the Avon. Looking at this Great Bath, with its diving stone, it is difficult to imagine Christ alive just a few years before Roman bathers first plunged into the warm water here. To assist with accuracy of date, there is a small fragment of stone cornice, dated A.D. 76 seen in the Roman Baths Museum.
Entering the enclosed East Baths, we found welcoming warmth in the spacious area, covered by an attractive cork accoustic ceiling. In semi-darkness our guide stepped through a railing, down to a Roman floor to fascinate us with descriptions of how the Romans enjoyed their Turkish baths. It is remarkable that remains of the Roman Bath did not attract attention until 1755, when Roman masonry was discovered after the demolition of a monastic building at the south-western corner of the Abbey.
It was in 1878, when repairs were being carried out, the discovery was made that houses were actually built over the Great Roman Bath. There is a photograph of one of these houses stand-

ing in this Bath, before being pulled down and the site excavated. We also know a Temple to Sul, patroness-deity of the springs, is near the Pump Room, and excavations are now being undertaken there.

While you are seeing the Roman Baths, you will enjoy the Museum with pewter tableware found in the spring, and its drain. This alloy was made of tin from Cornwall and lead from the nearby Mendip mines, and after being made into vessels in Bath this pewter was widely exported throughout Roman Britain.

An exciting discovery linking the wonders of our modern computer age with Roman life in Bath about 300 A.D. has been shown on our television screens. Pictures revealing measurements of the Temple taken over a number of years by Prof. Barry Cunliffe during excavations have been made possible by Dr. John Woodwark of Bath University. He has been able to make a three-dimensional computer model of the Temple and precinct, as they used to be. It is in full colour and includes people to give an idea of scale.

The Bath Evening Chronicle was so impressed when they first saw Dr. Woodwark's computer model, first produced for Professor Cunliffe, as his measurements of the ruins were fed in, that the newspaper commissioned a series of more detailed slides to include in the T.V. programme. Viewers even saw a view out of the Temple into the precinct as the Romans would have seen it. Now visitors to the Roman Baths can walk along this precinct on the ancient pavements many feet below our modern street level.

Refreshing themselves at the Baths, Roman citizens leisurely dined afterwards with the family or friends. They must have been in England quite a few years if they were to enjoy fruit from their apple trees brought over from Italy or France. It is interesting to wonder how they used cooking apples. I suggest the following recipes!

*

FESTIVAL APPLE TART

Make ¾ lb rich pastry and spread it on a buttered tart tin and make a few incisions here and there with a fork.
On top of the pastry arrange 2 lbs of apples peeled and cut in fine slices, adding about 4 oz castor sugar in between the layers of apple. Bake in a moderate oven for 30 minutes, 350°F (gas 4).
The apples should be slightly browned on the surface and moist inside. A little syrup, made from the peel of the apples, sugar, and a flavouring of either lemon peel, brandy, calvados, or sweet cider, can be poured over to form a glaze when the tart has cooled.

APPLE FRITTERS

Serves 4.
Dessert apples make the best fritters.
4 dessert apples; flour.
For the batter: 3 oz plain flour; pinch salt; 1 egg; 2 tablespoons water; 2 tablespoons milk.
Peel and core the apples, leaving them whole. Cut across into slices about ¼ in thick and place in a basin of cold satled water to prevent them from turning brown.
Sift the flour and salt for the batter into a mixing basin and make a well in the centre. Separate the egg, placing the yolk in the centre of the flour and the white in a mixing basin. Add the water and milk to the egg yolk. Mix them together and then gradually draw in the flour from around the sides of the basin to make a smooth batter. When ready to use beat the egg white until stiff and fold into the mixture.
Drain the apple slices, rinse in clear water and pat dry. Dust the slices with flour. This helps the batter to cling to the slices. Using a fork dip the apples into the batter. Allow excess batter to drain off and then lower the apple slices into about 1 in of

hot oil — you can do this in a frying pan. Fry for 2-3 minutes, turning to brown them on both sides. Then lift from the pan on to a sugared paper. Keep fritters warm in the oven, uncovered so they remain crisp while you cook the remainder. Serve sprinkled with sugar and pass cream separately.

HUNGARIAN APPLE TART

Ingredients: 4 large apples; 2 oz almonds; 2 oz sultanas, currants or raisins; squeeze of lemon juice; 2 oz sugar; 1 oz apricot jam; 6 to 8 oz shortcrust pastry — depending on size of tin.
Method: Make pastry and divide into two. Line 8″ tin with one piece. Peel, core and slice apples. Arrange half of apples on pastry then sultanas/currants/raisins, and the almonds and sugar, and jam. Arrange remaining apple on top, add squeeze of lemon. Roll and put on the top pastry, brush with milk or egg. Cook in oven 400°F (gas 6) for 20 to 30 minutes.
Then dredge with sugar and serve hot.

PRUNE AND APPLE PIE

Ingredients: 4 oz soaked and stoned prunes; 1½ lb cooking apples (peeled, cored and sliced); 4 oz soft brown sugar; 2 oz butter; 1 teaspoon cinnamon; 10 oz short crust pastry; milk to glaze.
Method: Place stoned prunes and apples in a pan with the sugar, butter and cinnamon. Cook gently until apples are just tender, stirring occasionally; leave to cool. Use half pastry to line an 8″ enamel or foil plate, spread in the filling, moisten edges with water and roll remaining pastry to cover. Press edges well together and flute.
Make small slits in centre, brush with milk and bake in hot oven 425°F (gas 7) for 30 to 40 minutes until brown.
Serve with cream, ice cream or custard.

BOTANICAL GARDENS

I entered the botanical gardens in Bath by the south gate, and was at once enfolded in a moist warmth between banks of alpines and shrubs, so tightly grown I sensed a delicious sweet-smelling security.
No-one was about. I strolled along the winding path. Seeing a wheelbarrow I then heard a scratching sound. Round the corner I saw white fan-tailed doves pecking bird seed, and close by in a shrubbery was a shed with a chimney pot. Was Beatrice Potter's famous character Mr. McGregor in his potting shed? No, instead Mr. George Langley emerged, and told me he had been finishing the Three Bears for his annual famous floral bed in Parade Gardens! He also told me the botanical gardens contain over 2,000 trees and shrubs within seven acres, the foliage renowned for dramatic autumn colours due to the limestone rock. Many botanists have visited these gardens since 1840, and today we are all welcome to ask advice about our own gardens.
I watched fish swimming in the pond, which is fed from water coming down from springs at Lansdown, while Mr. Langley told me Bathonians moving abroad often donate their ornamental fish for the pond. We saw a Muscovy duck nicknamed Dilly. Her bedraggled arrival at the Botanical Gardens only a month ago, was a mystery because Muscovy ducks do not fly. Now the duck's plumage is glossy with regular feeding.
Mr. Langley and I walked across to a tripetala magnolia tree, which has large simple leaves. These are sent to the Cheshire Home at Timsbury, where the handicapped residents use them to imprint into clay, which is then hand-painted and glazed. These finished dishes are shaped exactly like the leaves, and sell quickly providing an income for the men and women who enjoy making them.
Other leaves not wasted in the Botanical Gardens are the five-foot long leaves of the swamp plant, looking like gigantic rhubarb. These leaves act as reservoirs, catching rainwater, which then trickles down the stems. Gardeners place these leaves in

winter over the crowns to protect the plants against the cold.
We admired the beautiful magnolia leneii tree, now covered with white flowers turning pink. In autumn the green leaves become a brilliant red. I noticed other magnolia trees still producing flowers in June, which seemed unusual as I thought magnolia flowers lived a short life in May. Mr. Langley explained the pale pink flowers had a shorter life, but the deep pink magnolias continue to flower much longer.
When Mr. Langley mentioned Kew Gardens, near London, and the vast area that had to be covered, whereas in Bath's Botanical Gardens similar specimens could be seen, growing closer together, I recalled my childhood visits to Kew, when I lived in London, and how my small feet had ached!
We then looked at a special oriental fenel plant, which will later grow the tip of its leaves into shapes, like the strokes of a Chinese writer. Art students enjoy painting this plant.
One of the oldest rare trees is the tulip tree, which has saddle-shaped leaves and tulip-like flowers. In cold weather the bark sometimes splits and bleeds, requiring tree surgery. In fact the tree was bleeding when we looked closely, and not surprising, considering the chill of this June. We saw the tall blue foxglove tree, which has flowers like its name, and we gazed upwards to the top of two giant sequoia trees. In California they are the biggest trees in the world; one has a tunnel cut through the base of its trunk, through which runs a road. The biggest sequoias are over 2,000 years old, so it will be a long time before the Botanical Garden specimens in Bath endangers neighbouring trees.
At present the biggest tree in these gardens is the 130 ft. drooping lime, which happens to be the tallest in Great Britain. It has also a reputation for killing bees with drug type pollen. Thus, within seven acres Bath possesses tree giants that stand guard, warily conscious of each other, while dainty trees like the white-flowered crinoline of cornus controversa, Japanese acers, and tiny alpines cluster happily amongst rocks and enhance lawns.
Mr. Langely commented: 'While some visitors walk through the gardens in five minutes, others spend a day looking at these botanical gardens, to return again and again.'

Postscript: We later discovered through the local newspaper that Dilly the Muscovy duck had been left in the Botanical Gardens one night by a married couple who had found her ambling along their road. It seems nobody had wanted her, including the police, hence the respectable couple's furtive trip to the Botanical Gardens in an effort to find the duck a sanctuary. Bath is full of surprises.

PARADE GARDENS

When we have an English heat-wave, Bath can seem stifling. You may sigh: 'Oh for somewhere green and cool.'

I can recommend Parade Gardens in the heart of Bath, where you can escape to a place of cool serenity, sinking into a deckchair beneath trees and by flower beds that shimmer with colour. Musicians on the band stand entertain with melodious strains, and you can sip cool drinks to quench your thirst.

While you dreamily listen to the music, your eye may watch tiny birds pecking on the bandstand roof. Or gaze towards the chiselled turrets of Bath Abbey, sunlit against the sky. Small children play contentedly on the lawns, while their mothers chat.

A delightful way to spend a couple of hours, before setting off once again to discover Bath.

Whilst gardeners from all over the world visit Bath's Botanical Gardens to admire rare and exotic plants, many of us are content in town or country gardens growing soft fruits and apples to eat through winter, and we are proud of our vegetable plots. Here are typical recipes using the harvest of our labours!

*

BEETROOT CHUTNEY

Ingredients: 1 lb cored and chopped apples; 3 lb chopped, small beetroots; 1 lb chopped onions; 3 cloves chopped garlic; 4 oz sultanas; 1 pt spiced white vinegar; 1 lb granulated sugar; 2 teaspoons salt.

Method: Cook onions in a little vinegar to soften a little and then add rest of ingredients. Cook gently and stir continuously to prevent sticking. When soft add the sugar and the remainder of the vinegar. Cook slowly for ½ hour. Put into hot jars. Seal when cold.

RED CABBAGE WITH APPLE

Serves 4.
1 small red cabbage, about 1½ lb; 1 oz butter; 1 medium-sized onion; 2 large cooking apples; salt and freshly milled pepper; 1-2 tablespoons demerara sugar; juice of ½ lemon.
Quarter the cabbage and cut away the core. Shred the cabbage across finely. Wash in cold water. Melt the butter in a large saucepan and add the peeled and finely chopped onion. Cook gently for a few minutes until the onion softens, then pack the cabbage into the pan. Add sufficient boiling water to cover the base of the pan — about 1 in. in depth.
Peel, core and cut up the apples and add also season with salt and freshly milled pepper, then add the sugar and lemon juice. Stir to mix well. Cover with a lid and simmer gently for 3-4 hours. Red cabbage should be cooked slowly. Keep the pan tightly covered; once the apples begin to pulp down no more water should be required. Stir occasionally and towards the end of the cooking time taste and add more sugar or lemon juice. Serve hot with roast pork or duck.

APPLE & BLACKBERRY COMPOTE

Serves 6.
Ingredients: 6 oz sugar; ½ pint water; 1 lb blackberries; 1 lb dessert apples; 1 level tablespoon cornflour.
Method: Measure the sugar and water into a saucepan. Stir over low heat until the sugar has dissolved, then bring up to the boil and simmer for 1 minute. Meanwhile, peel, core and slice the apples. Wash the blackberries. Add the apples to the saucepan and cover with a lid. Simmer gently for 1 minute, then add the blackberries. Bring back to the boil and draw the pan off the heat. Leave the pan covered with a lid to stand for about 15 minutes, or until the fruit is tender.
Either strain, or carefully remove, the fruit from the syrup using a perforated spoon. Place the fruit in a serving dish and return

the juice to the saucepan. Blend the cornflour with a little cold water and stir into the fruit juice. Bring up to the boil, stirring until slightly thickened, and clear. Pour the juice over the fruit. Cool, then chill well before serving.
Serve with cream.

FRUIT CHUTNEY

Ingredients: 4 lb cooking apples; 1 lb pears; 1 lb plums; 3 lb red tomatoes; ½ lb sultanas; ½ lb seedless raisins; 3½ to 4 lb demerara sugar; 3½ to 4 pts vinegar; 2 tablespoons salt; 1 teaspoon mace; 1 teaspoon cayenne; 1 teaspoon cloves; 1 teaspoon peppercorns; 1 teaspoon ground ginger.
Method: Plunge tomatoes into boiling water to remove skins; then slice them. Chop apples, plums and pears. Put everything into a pan, bring to boil slowly and simmer for 2 hours. The cloves and peppercorns should be tied in a muslin bag and removed before potting.

* * *

WASSAILING
Here's to thee, old apple tree,
Whence thou may'st bud
And whence thou may'st blow,
and whence thou may'st bear apple anew.
Hats full, caps full,
and our pockets full, too.
Huzza! Huzza! Huzza!

HUNTING FOR ANTIQUES

Bathonians, and visitors too, cannot resist looking in the many antique shop windows. Why are there so many shops here selling fine furniture, China and curios? Probably because Regency furnishings complement the tall, elegant rooms of Georgian houses. Also one considers many residents live to ninety, and during their life have accumulated pieces that have been handed down in the family to them. They may well outlive nearest relations, and so finally their homes are cleared and the contents auctioned often to replenish the stock in antique shops. For the younger housewife there is much satisfaction in becoming the proud owner of a mahogany table, which has acquired a beautiful depth of colour, the patina, through many years of careful polishing. Browsing in such shops over the years, my home gleams with brass and copper, and a love of old prints has become a joke in the family, for one can run out of wall space!
It is an event to visit Guinea Lane Market. Walk along the Paragon and turn left up steep steps, as indicated by a large poster. When I entered this market, swirling shapes of art nouveau decorated the walls, and ornate Victorian furniture was admired to the background music of 'West Side Story'. All somewhat bewildering, but especially interesting when you see the dealers, who may be elegant and lively, middle-aged and doleful or long-haired and hopeful. These men and women have tempting trays of bric-à-brac, silver, China, furniture and pieces of old lace. I still wistfully think of the armchair I didn't buy, with its frame of smooth inlaid mahogany.
If you like such things I am sure you will also enjoy a visit to the Great Western Antique Centre in Barlett Street and the old established Guildhall Market. Alternatively, you may visit Jolly's famous Auction Rooms in Old King's Street, and Powell and Powell's Auctions in Princes Buildings, both near Milsom Street. When one considers fine antiques, older Bathonians will remember seeing the Queen's grandmother, the late Queen Mary, strolling round Bath in the last war, and making her purchases in

the antique shops, often with the Dowager Duchess of Gloucester, who was then a young woman. I wish you happy hunting, dear readers.

Hunting for antiques can be hungry work!

*

GAMMON & CIDER & APPLES

Serves 6.
1 piece gammon or bacon, about 2-2½ lb; 1½-2 lb cooking apples; 1 small onion, stuck with a clove; bay leaf; 1 pint dry cider; 1 tablespoon sugar; ½ oz butter.
The top: 1 teaspoon French mustard; 2-3 tablespoons demerara sugar; few whole cloves.
Soak the gammon for several hours in cold water. Peel, core and quarter the apples and arrange over the base of a large saucepan. Add the onion stuck with the clove and the bay leaf. Set the piece of gammon on top of the apples and add the cider; it should be just sufficient to cover the apples. Cover the pan and bring up to the boil. Simmer gently allowing 30 minutes per lb. Lift the gammon from the pan, using a small sharp knife, strip away the rind. Score the fat in a criss-cross pattern. Spread with the mustard, then coat with the demerara sugar and finally stick in a few cloves. Set in a roasting tin, place in the centre of a moderately hot oven, 400°F (gas 6) and bake for 15-20 minutes, until glazed and brown.

Meanwhile strain off the cooking liquor, reserving the apples. Remove the onion and bay leaf and return the apples to the saucepan. Stir to break them up to a purée and add the sugar and butter. Heat gently, allowing any excess moisture to boil away. Serve the apple sauce with the sliced gammon.

WAGGON-WHEEL CAKE

Ingredients: 1 packet (3 oz) Philadelphia Cheese; 1 oz soft margarine; 4 oz castor sugar; grated rind of 1 lemon; 2 eggs (beaten); 4 oz self-raising flour; ¼ teaspoon baking powder.
Topping: 2 dessert apples; 1 tablespoon lemon juice; 1 tablespoon castor sugar.
Beat cheese and margarine together, add sugar and beat until light and fluffy. Add lemon rind and egg, a little at a time, beating well. Sieve flour and baking powder and fold into creamed mixture. Turn into a greased (8") sandwich tin and smooth top.
Peel, core and slice apples, and sprinkle with lemon juice. Arrange apple slices over cake mixture to form a waggon-wheel pattern, pressing core edge ½" down into mixture. Sprinkle over tablespoon castor sugar and cook at 350°F (gas 4) for 50-60 minutes. Leave in tin for 10 minutes to cool. Sprinkle with castor sugar and serve warm or cold with cream.

APPLE WHAT-NOT PUDDING

Ingredients: Base — 1 lb cooking apples; 1 oz butter; 1 oz sugar; grated rind of lemon.
Sauce — 1 standard egg; 1 oz butter; 1 oz plain flour; 1 oz sugar; three-quarters pint milk.
Topping: 2 oz demerara sugar; ½ teaspoon cinnamon; ½ oz butter.
Method: Peel, core and slice apples. Place butter in a saucepan and melt. Add apples and sugar. Cover and cook over low heat stirring occasionally until soft and thick. Remove heat and stir in lemon rind. Spread in 1½ pt. oven-proof dish.
Melt butter, stir in flour and cook gently. Add milk and bring to boil, stirring, and simmer for 2 minutes. Remove from heat and stir in sugar. Gradually stir in beaten egg. Return to heat and cook 1 minute stirring. Pour sauce over apple.
Prepare medium grill. Mix brown sugar and cinnamon together.

Sprinkle on top of sauce and dot with butter. Place dish under grill and heat until sugar has caramelised. Serve hot or cold.

APPLE DUMPLINGS

Serves 4.
Short-crust pastry using 8 oz flour and 4 oz butter or use 12 oz ready-made pastry; 4 medium-sized cooking apples; brown sugar; butter; pinch of grated nutmeg or ground cloves.
Peel and core the apples. Roll the pastry into a rectangle about quarter inch thick. Cut it into four squares. Put an apple on each piece and fill the centre with sugar. Add a knob of butter and a pinch of either of the spices. Moisten the edges of the pastry with water and then mould it up over the apple, making a good seal at the top. Turn the dumpling upside-down on a baking tray and cook until the pastry is crisp, 400°F (gas 6) 30 minutes approximately, and the apple feels soft when you pierce it with a fine skewer. Serve hot or cold with custard or cream.

* * *

Coleridge holds that a man cannot have a pure mind who refuses apple-dumplings. I am not certain but he is right.
Charles Lamb (1775-1834)

GHOST HOOVES BRIDGE A CHASM OF 300 YEARS

I had a marvellous time following up stories after my request for ghostly whereabouts from readers of the Bath Evening Chronicle. Strangely, all the Bath ghosts relate to the Battle of Lansdown, fought between the Royalists and Roundheads on 5th July 1643. Mr. Henderson invited me to his home Merthyr Villa, Newbridge Hill, where the ghostly presence of a young woman is felt by him and his wife. She nursed soldiers after the Battle of Lansdown, when they rested in the villa. Remarkably, her ghost also visits Derwent House, a few yards along the Kelston Road, where other soldiers were nursed by her.

At the time of the Civil War, Derwent House was owned by a doctor surgeon, who attended Sir Bevil Grenville, when he fell mortally injured during the Battle of Lansdown. The young nurse's ghost has twice been mentioned in the deeds of Derwent House with an interval of one hundred years. Since she is felt to trip light-heartedly through both houses, no-one is worried by her presence.

A psychic lady once visited Merthyr Villa, and on entering the front door could immediately tell the owner where the ghost walked, and the window through which she would gaze, this being a small window on the righthand side of the front door looking on Newbridge Hill.

When I walked through the house I perhaps imagined it chill in the hall, but otherwise it was a happy house. Mr. Henderson indicated the whereabouts of a huge fireplace in which six men could stand. He had boarded this up to make the house warmer, but we could still feel the stone lintel on which were scratch marks, supposed to have been made by soldiers on the eve of the Battle as they sharpened their axes. I also descended a circular stone staircase to a cellar, where Roundhead prisoners were kept for the night after the battle.

After my visit I read in the Library an account of the battle, in which the Roundheads 'sent a whole body of horse and dragoons down the hill to charge the rear and flank of the King's forces, which they did thoroughly; the regiment of cavalrymen so terrorising the King's horses that they would not charge'.

Now I will tell you of another reader's letter which came from Mrs. King of Sydney Road, in which she wrote of her friendship with a young woman, when they were both cooks at Beech House in 1914, where there were convalescent soldiers injured during the First World War.

Mrs. King's friend lived with her parents at Battlefields House just below Landsdown, on the road to Wick. It seems within a few weeks of living in the house the young friend's parents awoke one night to hear horses clattering down the drive. This being 1914 they rushed downstairs to see what had happened to their horses, and they were very surprised to find these horses safe in the stables. There was no trace of any horse having raced down the drive!

When the parents visited people in Wick for tea, a few weeks later, the host after listening to their strange account said: 'Every family that comes to Battlefields House has this experience. It only happens once. What you heard can be supposed to be riderless horses that fled from the Battle of Lansdown. The drive of Battlefields House was then a road, and the horses were rushing to escape.'

How most extraordinary that my ghost enquiries should have brought such related information from Mr. Henderson and Mrs. King, who were unknown to one another.

Ghosts always seem to have lost their appetite – have you ever seen one tucking into his dinner!

*

HERRINGS WITH APPLE SALAD

Serves 4.

1 medium-sized onion; 2 dessert apples; juice of ½ lemon; 1

carton soured cream; salt and freshly milled pepper; 4 pickled herrings.

Peel the onion leaving it whole. Slice into rings and place in a mixing basin. Cover with boiling water and allow to soak for 2 minutes. Drain and chill.

Peel and core the apple and dice into a basin. Sprinkle with the lemon juice and toss the apple pieces. Add the onions rings, the soured cream and a seasoning of salt and pepper. Toss the ingredients to mix.

Drain the herrings from any liquor and open out. Arrange the herrings flat on individual serving dishes with the flesh side uppermost. Spoon the apple and onion and soured cream mixture over the top and serve with green salad.

APPLE CREAM FLAN

Pastry — 4 oz plain flour; 3 oz margarine; 1 tablespoon water; 1 oz castor sugar; pinch of salt.

Custard — 2 eggs; 1 oz plain flour; 2 oz sugar; ½ pt. milk; vanilla essence.

Topping — 2 tablespoons warmed, sieved apricot jam; 1 oz castor sugar; ½ oz browned flaked almonds; ½ lb cooking apples;

Method: Make pastry and line 7" greased flan ring. Prick base. Blend eggs, sugar and flour in a bowl. Bring milk to boil and add slowly to egg mixture. Return to pan and cook gently for 1 minute, stirring all the time. Remove from heat and add vanilla essence.

Spread custard in flan case and arrange very thin slices of apple in a circular pattern. Sprinkle with 1 oz sugar. Bake in a hot oven for 30 minutes, 375°F (gas 5). Spoon over glaze and almonds.

SPICY APPLE CAKES

Ingredients: 8 oz self-raising flour; 2 level teaspoons baking powder; 4 oz butter; 5 oz castor sugar; 2 eggs; 6 oz cooking apples, finely chopped; 1 level teaspoon nutmeg; 1 level teaspoon cinnamon; 2 tablespoons milk.

Method: Sieve flour and baking powder; cream and 4 oz sugar until light and fluffy. Add eggs gradually, beating well. Stir in apple and half the nutmeg and half the cinnamon. Fold in flour and milk. Spoon into cases. Mix remaining sugar with remaining spices and sprinkle a little on the top of each cake. Bake at 400°F (gas 6) for 15-20 minutes.

APPLE FILLER CHEESE

Mix 1 oz flour, 1 teaspoon cinnamon, grated rind of 1 lemon and 3 oz brown sugar together. Cream 4 oz Philadelphia cream cheese until soft and beat in one quarter pint of milk. Whisk all together to form a thin batter.
Peel, core and slice 1 lb apples. Arrange in layers in shallow ovenproof dish — sprinkle with lemon juice. Pour on batter. Sprinkle 1 oz demerara sugar on top. Bake at 375°F (gas 5) for 30-35 minutes until set.

* * *

But I, when I undress me
Each night, upon my knees
Will ask the Lord to bless me
With apple pie and cheese
                           Eugene Field (1850-1895)

COUNTRY STROLL IN OLD WIDCOMBE

I would like to take you on a walk around one of the prettiest places just a couple of miles from the centre of Bath. Hopefully it will be as sunny a morning as when my country walk in Widcombe started at the bottom of Ralph Allen's Drive, and I set off down Church Lane. Even the birds seemed to sing more brightly down there, and my thoughts went back to the time I was a bride and lived in Widcombe Terrace.

I remembered my young husband taking me for a midnight walk down Church Lane one hot, summer night. It was all the more fun because I was a London girl, and unaware of nightlife among animals and birds. When we heard an owl and my husband hooted softly in reply, I was sure the bird would swoop down on us! How still Widcombe Manor, Manor Farm and St. Thomas à Becket Church seemed in the moonlight. When we walked up the lane at the back of the church, a badger had padded along in the shadows beside us.

Now in the bright autumn morning sunshine I paused outside the Manor to watch white doves preening themselves on the roof. Whippets ran about in front of the house, just as I had seen them several years earlier, but their muzzles were whitening with age. Gargoyles on the Manor's walls still smiled or mocked, according to your mood. Widcombe Manor, built in 1727, reflected the days of 'Tom Jones', when country squires were lusty and robust, and ladies tripped into the gardens to pick roses, their long dresses billowing, and sun-hats caught beneath the chin with ribbons. Henry Fielding, author of 'Tom Jones', actually lived next door in Widcombe Lodge. His character Squire Allworthy in this famous novel was inspired by Ralph Allen, who resided in nearby Prior Park College.

Not long after my marriage Princess Margaret and Tony Armstrong Jones, later to become Lord Snowdon, used to stay with friends in Widcombe Manor, about the time they were newly wed. Close by the Manor and Widcombe Lodge, the parish church St. Thomas à Becket looked so settled in the grassy

churchyard it might always have been there! Inside I stood in the chapel, where our daughter had been christened, and read it was the site of an original Anglo Saxon church before 983 A.D. Indeed a perpetual comfort and conscience to men long before Widcombe Manor was built.

Closing the heavy door behind, I walked up the lane behind the church, and could see its weather cock set towards another weather-vane nearby on Manor Farm. White doves flocked together on the farm's roof, assuredly the Manor doves' relations. Grey squirrels raced high in nearby trees at the sound of my footsteps. Further up the lane I came to Strawberry Gardens, a cottage which was once an inn, called the Ring o' Bells. It has been said smugglers rested there, after coming over the hills and down the nearby bridle path with pack horses laden with brandy and silks for Bath. A romantic thought. I crossed the lane and noticed old yew trees had been cut down to open a panoramic view of Prior Park College, set high upon the hill in rolling green countryside. Below I could see someone fishing in the lake by the Palladian Bridge.

Too soon it was time for me to leave this rural tranquility, and return to the City walking down Widcome Hill this time, and turning right into Pulteney Road. Passing beneath the railway bridge, I turned left towards North Parade and the Recreation Ground. Near the small bridge spanning the Avon I descended steps to the tow-path facing Pulteney Bridge. Together with the rushing flow of water and landscaped gardens I enjoyed looking towards the tiny shops of Pulteney Bridge, especially the coffee shop where I knew their coffee from Brazil to be particularly good, and I could almost smell the roasted coffee beans!

NOTES